"Hey, God"

"Hey, God"

Daniel Sanzhura

XULON PRESS

Xulon Press
2301 Lucien Way #415
Maitland, FL 32751
407.339.4217
www.xulonpress.com

© 2019 by Daniel Sanzhura

All rights reserved solely by the author. The author guarantees all contents are original and do not infringe upon the legal rights of any other person or work. No part of this book may be reproduced in any form without the permission of the author. The views expressed in this book are not necessarily those of the publisher.

Unless otherwise indicated, Scripture quotations taken from the King James Version (KJV) – *public domain.*

Scripture quotations taken from the New King James Version (NKJV). Copyright © 1982 by Thomas Nelson, Inc. Used by permission. All rights reserved.

Scripture quotations taken from the English Standard Version (ESV). Copyright © 2001 by Crossway, a publishing ministry of Good News Publishers. Used by permission. All rights reserved.

Scripture quotations taken from the Holy Bible, New International Version (NIV). Copyright © 1973, 1978, 1984, 2011 by Biblica, Inc.™. Used by permission. All rights reserved.

Scripture quotations taken from the New American Standard Bible (NASB). Copyright © 1960, 1962, 1963, 1968, 1971, 1972, 1973, 1975, 1977, 1995 by The Lockman Foundation. Used by permission. All rights reserved.

Printed in the United States of America.
ISBN-13: 978-1-54566-139-0

Read this book in its entirety.

In this life there's a variety of important topics to cover:
this book covers money, family, church, and the end times.

Money

No; most people don't really understand the importance of money. I wish more people spoke more on this topic. According to a CNBC news article titled *Most Americans Live Paycheck to Paycheck*, seventy-eight percent of Americans live paycheck to paycheck, and seventy-one percent of all US workers say they're now in debt (www.cnbc.com/2017/08/24/most-americans-live-paycheck-to-paycheck.html).

Why that many? You might wonder. *What is the reason?* It's because people haven't been told. They haven't been informed. Money is one of the biggest reasons why people have problems in life, aside from having to deal with sickness or an accident a person with money problems is a person with a lot of problems!

The person whose finances are in order and who controls his money is above his money; he or she is not flooded by debt. Money is so important. It's one of the most important aspects of life a person needs to understand because money dictates work, lifestyle, food, clothes, cars, gas, homes, schools, and the world we live in. All of these needs in life are provided for by money, and if you understand and can control money, you will see how to navigate through life. You'll know where to live, where not to live, what car to buy, and what car not to buy. You'll understand the lifestyle you can and can't comfortably live. Once you gain knowledge about money, you will know and see things you didn't before. Money is a guiding tool for our lives here on earth.

There does come a security and peace of mind from having money because money fills the void between what you don't want and what you do want. Speaking of earthly things like wanting a house or wanting some food, money can fix that. Not wanting creditors to call or have your car repossessed, money can fix that. Want less marital problems? Money can fix that.

The Bible commands us not to trust in riches, and this book is about obeying what the Bible commands. Here's a short list of scriptures from the book of Proverbs that speak about money:

> Joyful is the person who finds wisdom, the one who gains understanding. For wisdom is more profitable than silver and her wages are better than gold. (Proverbs 3:13,14)

> Choose my instruction rather than silver, and knowledge rather than pure gold. For wisdom is far more valuable than rubies. Nothing you desire can compare with it. (Proverbs 8:10, 11)

MONEY

Better to have a little with fear for the Lord,
then to have great treasure and inner turmoil.
(Proverbs 15:16)

Take a lesson from the ants, you lazybones.
Learn from their ways and become wise!
Though they have no prince or governor or
ruler to make them work, they labor hard
all summer, gathering food for the winter.
(Proverbs 6:6-8)

A wise youth harvests in the Summer but
one who sleeps during harvest is a disgrace.
(Proverbs 10:5)

A hard worker has plenty of food, but a
person who chases fantasies has no sense.
(Proverbs 12:11)

Those who mock the poor insult their Maker.
Those who rejoice at the misfortune of others
will be punished. (Proverbs 17:5)

"Hey, God"

The rich think of their wealth as a strong defense they imagine it to be a high wall of safety. (Proverbs 28:3)

A poor person who oppresses the poor is like a pounding rain that destroys the crops. (Proverbs 18:11)

Trust in the Lord with all your heart, do not lean on your own understanding. Seek his will in all you do, and he will show you which path to take. (Proverbs 3:5, 6)

People curse those who hoard their grain, but they bless the one who sells in time of need. (Proverbs 11:26)

Those who trust in their riches will fall but the righteous will thrive like a green leaf. (Proverbs 11:28)

O God, I beg two favors from You, let Me have them before I die. First, help me never to tell a lie. Second, give me neither poverty nor riches! Give me just enough to satisfy my

> needs. For if I grow rich, I may deny you and say, "Who is the Lord?" and if I am poor, I may steal and thus insult God's holy name. (Proverbs 30:7-9)

This is what Jesus said to his disciples:

> And again, I say unto you. It is easier for a camel to go through the eye of a needle, than for a rich man to enter in to the kingdom of GOD! When his disciples heard it, they were exceedingly amazed, saying Who then can be saved. But Jesus beheld them and said unto them, with men this is impossible, but with God all things are possible. (Matthew 19:24-26)

What we want is to be a wise man, not a rich one: wise in your finances, wise in your business decisions, wise in your marriage, wise in your church—wise in all areas of life. God wants His children to be wise. There are thousands of books on managing money, and the focus of these books is always on money as the problem. The problem is not money; the problem is the person. It's important to not fall in love with money. Instead, be obedient to what God says about what a person should be. Again, God wants us to be a wise man, not a rich one.

Family

Malachi addresses fundamental problems in Israel's society that are also prevalent in our society today. The lack of responsibility fathers are assuming toward their children. In our generation so many girls are having promiscuous sex, getting pregnant, and then having to abort those babies. Also, not counting those girls sleeping around that don't end up needing abortions, so many kids being born as bastard children—you have your parents to thank for that. Girls nowadays have no shame, no elegance. Boys are growing up but they're not becoming men. The next generation doesn't need to pass their parents sins on. God created marriage for a good purpose to have a good healthy family. A husband, a wife, then children, in order to leave a decent legacy. This is where being a father plays a big role.

Fathers in the White House, fathers in government buildings, fathers in police stations, fathers in schools, even fathers in churches have left their posts in the family, particularly their post with their children, in pursuit of recognition from their jobs, their peers, and their superiors, while their children are left to their mothers to care for and to provide answers.

Fathers must reclaim their role of being a father because they're not raising their children. The mothers are bitter at the fathers for not raising them, and who's responsible? Nobody knows. Nobody cares. That's not what God had in mind for a family: "*Fathers train up a child in the way he should go, and when he is old, he will not depart from it*" (Prov. 22:6, NKJV).

In the book of Malachi in the Old Testament, God says He will send Elijah the prophet before the dreadful day of the Lord. While this hasn't yet occurred, Jesus hasn't yet come a second time, He came the first time, and before Jesus comes again, Elijah will come:

> *Behold, I will send you Elijah the prophet, Before the coming of the great and dreadful day of the LORD. And he will turn the hearts of the fathers to the children, and the hearts of the children to their fathers, Lest I come and strike the earth with a curse.* (Malachi 4: 5-6)

Worldwide there's an estimated forty- to fifty-million abortions every year. That's approximately 125,000 abortions every day.

> "*Fathers train up a child in the way he should go, and when he is old, he will not depart from it*" (Prov. 22:6, NKJV).

Where are our fathers? They're certainly not assuming responsibility for their daughters, or this abortion epidemic might not be happening today.

Malachi continues on dealing treacherously with your wife in 2:13-16. God hates divorce:

> *And this is the second thing you do: You cover the altar of the LORD with tears, with weeping and crying; So, He does not regard the offering anymore, nor receive it with goodwill from your hands. Yet you say, "For what reason?" Because the LORD has been witness Between you and the wife of your youth, with whom you have dealt treacherously; yet she is your companion and your wife by covenant. But did He not make them one, having a remnant of the Spirit? And why one? He seeks godly offspring. Therefore, take heed to your spirit, and let none deal treacherously with the wife of his youth. For the LORD God of Israel says that He hates divorce, For it covers one's garment with violence," says the LORD of hosts. "Therefore, take heed to your spirit, that you do not deal treacherously."*

TITHES
AND OFFERINGS

"Will a man rob God? Yet you have robbed Me! But you say, 'In what way have we robbed You?' In tithes and offerings. You are cursed with a curse, for you have robbed Me, even this whole nation. Bring all the tithes into the storehouse, that there may be food in My house, and try Me now in this," says the LORD of hosts, "If I will not open for you the windows of heaven and pour out for you such blessing that there will not be room enough to receive it. And I will rebuke the devourer for your sakes, so that he will not destroy the fruit of your ground, nor shall the vine fail to bear fruit for you in the field," says the LORD of hosts; "And all nations will call you blessed, for you will be a delightful land," says the LORD of hosts. (Malachi 3:8-12)

> *Each of you should give what you have decided in your heart to give, not reluctantly or under compulsion, for God loves a cheerful giver.* (2 Corinthians 9:7, NIV)

It's more common for the head of the household to tithe. And it's appropriate in the family for every man to decide upon tithing for the family. Tithing is more than giving to the pastor; it's giving to God, and tithing should be approached as giving God a valuable offering willingly. As we know, God gave His best to us, His Son Jesus, our Lord and Savior, and Jesus gave Himself for us.

A Book of Remembrance

> *Then those who feared the LORD spoke to one another, and the LORD listened and heard them; so, a book of remembrance was written before Him for those who fear the LORD and who meditate on His name. "They shall be Mine," says the LORD of hosts, "On the day that I make them My jewels. And I will spare them as a man spares his own son who serves him." Then you shall again discern between the righteous and the wicked, between one who serves God and one who does not serve Him.* (Malachi 3:16-18)

God addresses the heart of the matter on tithing in Malachi:

"To you priests who despise My name. Who is there even among you who would shut the doors, so that you would not kindle fire on My altar in vain? I have no pleasure in you," says the LORD of hosts, "Nor will I accept an offering from your hands. For from the rising of the sun, even to its going down, My name shall be great among the Gentiles; In every place incense shall be offered to My name, and a pure offering; for My name shall be great among the nations," says the LORD of hosts. "But you profane it, in that you say, 'The table of the LORD is defiled; and its fruit, its food, is contemptible.' You also say, 'Oh, what a weariness!' and you sneer at it," says the LORD of hosts. "And you bring the stolen, the lame, and the sick; thus, you bring an offering! Should I accept this from your hand?" says the LORD. "But cursed be the deceiver who has in his flock a male, and takes a vow, but sacrifices to the Lord what is blemished–for I am a great King," says the LORD of hosts, "and My name is to be feared among the nations." (Malachi 1:10-14)

In the twenty-first century we don't bring fruit and goats to the Lord but give our tithes and offerings, and giving stolen or "dirty" money is just as evil as offering God a lame or sick animal in Malachi's time. Should He accept that from your hand? *"'But cursed be the deceiver who has in his flock a male, and takes a vow, but sacrifices to the Lord what is blemished–for I am a great King,' says the LORD of hosts, 'And My name is to be feared among the nations'"* (Mal. 1:14).

CHURCH

Church is so important. Believers cannot grow as Christians by themselves. The church is to the Christian what the mother is to a child.

A person's Christian maturity is evident by their obedience to God. If you think about Jesus's life on earth, the Bible says that He was obedient to death, even death on a cross. True godly obedience is being Isaac and getting on the altar Abraham made. Jesus was obedient unto death, even death on a cross (Phil. 2:8). God want's that kind of obedience. Understand the sacrifice Christ made for us. Do you see a person's maturity by their obedience? How far are you willing to be obedient to God?

The point here is death. While we will most likely not be expected to die for the gospel of Jesus, we will die someday — if Jesus doesn't return first.. Are we obedient as Jesus was? Are we ready for that day?

The analogy is given of a human body if you aren't part of the body how can you grow? Christ being the head.

> So I made up my mind that I would not make
> another painful visit to you. For if I grieve you,

who is left to make me glad but you whom I have grieved? I wrote as I did, so that when I came, I would not be distressed by those who should have made me rejoice. I had confidence in all of you, that you would all share my joy. For I wrote you out of great distress and anguish of heart and with many tears, not to grieve you but to let you know the depth of my love for you. (2 Corinthians 2:1-4, NIV)

Forgiveness for the Offender

If anyone has caused grief, he has not so much grieved me as he has grieved all of you to some extent—not to put it too severely. The punishment inflicted on him by the majority is sufficient. Now instead, you ought to forgive and comfort him, so that he will not be overwhelmed by excessive sorrow. I urge you, therefore, to reaffirm your love for him. Another reason I wrote you was to see if you would stand the test and be obedient in everything. Anyone you forgive, I also forgive. And what I have forgiven—if there was anything to forgive—I have forgiven in the sight of Christ for your sake, in order that Satan might not outwit us. For we are not unaware of his schemes. (2 Corinthians 2:5-11)

Ministers of the New Covenant

Now when I went to Troas to preach the gospel of Christ and found that the Lord had opened a door for me, I still had no peace of mind, because I did not find my brother Titus there. So, I said goodbye to them and went on to Macedonia.

But thanks be to God, who always leads us as captives in Christ's triumphal procession and uses us to spread the aroma of the knowledge of him everywhere. For we are to God the pleasing aroma of Christ among those who are being saved and those who are perishing. To the one we are an aroma that brings death; to the other, an aroma that brings life. And who is equal to such a task? Unlike so many, we do not peddle the word of God for profit. On the contrary, in Christ we speak before God with sincerity, as those sent from God. *(2 Corinthians 2:12-17)*

For many walk, of whom I have told you often, and now tell you even weeping, that they are the enemies of the cross of Christ: Whose end is destruction, whose God is their belly, and whose glory is in their shame, who

> mind earthly things.) For our conversation is in heaven; from whence also we look for the Savior, the Lord Jesus Christ: Who shall change our vile body, that it may be fashioned like unto his glorious body, according to the working whereby he is able even to subdue all things unto himself. (Philippians 3:18-21)

All this is from God, who reconciled us to himself through Christ and gave us the ministry of reconciliation: that God was reconciling the world to himself in Christ, not counting people's sins against them. And he has committed to us the message of reconciliation.

We are therefore Christ's ambassadors, as though God were making his appeal through us. We implore you on Christ's behalf: Be reconciled to God.

Picture a body and picture all of us inside that one body. In that body of Jesus, we have the mind of Christ. We have different functions in that body but one mind, one head: the Lord Jesus Christ. With that image in mind, consider the following scripture verses from Ephesians 2:19-22. These help us understand our position as Christ's body:

> So then you are no longer strangers and aliens, but you are fellow citizens with the saints and members of the household of God, built on the foundation of the apostles and prophets, Christ Jesus himself being the cornerstone,

in whom the whole structure, being joined together, grows into a holy temple in the Lord. In him you also are being built together into a dwelling place for God by the Spirit.

Instead, speaking the truth in love, we are to grow up in every way into him who is the head, into Christ, from whom the whole body, joined and held together by every joint with which it is equipped, when each part is working properly, makes the body grow so that it builds itself up in love. (Ephesians 4:15-16)

Then the church throughout Judea, Galilee and Samaria enjoyed a time of peace and was strengthened. Living in the fear of the Lord and encouraged by the Holy Spirit, it increased in numbers. (Acts 9:31-32)

For no one ever hated his own flesh, but nourishes and cherishes it, just as Christ does the church, because we are members of his body. (Ephesians 5:29-30)

And let us consider how we may spur one another on toward love and good deeds, not giving up meeting together, as some are in the habit of doing, but encouraging one another—and all the more as you see the Day approaching. (Hebrews 10:24-25)

Therefore, laying aside falsehood, SPEAK TRUTH EACH ONE of you WITH HIS NEIGBOR, for we are members of one another. (Ephesians 4:25, emphasis mine)

Now you are Christ's body, and individually members of it. For even as the body is one and yet has many members, and all the members of the body, though they are many, are one body, so also is Christ. For by one Spirit we were all baptized into one body, whether Jews or Greeks, whether slaves or free, and we were all made to drink of one Spirit. (1 Corinthians 12:27)

Be ye therefore followers of God, as dear children; And walk in love, as Christ also hath loved us, and hath given himself for us an offering and a sacrifice to God for a sweet-smelling savor. But fornication, and all uncleanness, or covetousness, let it not be once named among you, as becometh saints; Neither filthiness, nor foolish talking, nor jesting, which are not convenient: but rather giving of thanks. For this ye know, that no whoremonger, nor unclean person, nor covetous man, who is an idolater, hath any inheritance in the kingdom of Christ and of God. Let no man deceive you with vain words: for because of these things cometh the wrath of God upon the children of disobedience. Be not ye therefore partakers with them. For ye were sometimes darkness, but now are ye light in the Lord: walk as children of light: (For the fruit of the Spirit is in all goodness and righteousness and truth;) Proving what is acceptable unto the Lord. And have no fellowship with the unfruitful works of darkness, but rather reprove them. For it is a shame even to speak of those things which are done of them in secret. But all things that are reproved are made manifest by the light: for whatsoever doth make manifest is light. Wherefore he saith, awake thou that sleepest, and arise from the dead, and Christ shall give thee light. See then that ye walk circumspectly, not as fools, but as wise, Redeeming the time, because the days are evil. Wherefore be ye not unwise but understanding what the will of the Lord is. And be not drunk with wine, wherein is excess; but be filled with the Spirit; speaking to yourselves in psalms and hymns and spiritual songs, singing and making melody in your heart to the Lord; Giving thanks always for all things unto God and the Father in the name of our Lord Jesus Christ; Submitting yourselves one to another in the fear of God. (Ephesians 5:1-21)

Now concerning virgins, I have no commandment of the Lord: yet I give my judgment, as one that hath obtained mercy of the Lord to be faithful. I suppose therefore that this is good for the present distress, I say, that it is good for a man so to be. Art, thou bound unto a wife? seek not to be loosed. Art, thou loosed from a wife? Seek not a wife. But and if thou marry, thou hast not sinned; and if a virgin marries, she hath not sinned. Nevertheless, such shall have trouble in the flesh: but I spare you. But this I say, brethren, the time is short: it remaineth, that both they that have wives be as though they had none; And they that weep, as though they wept not; and they that rejoice, as though they rejoiced not; and they that buy, as though they possessed not; And they that use this world, as not abusing it: for the fashion of this world passes away. (1 Corinthians 7:25-31)

Moreover, brethren, I would not that ye should be ignorant, how that all our fathers were under the cloud, and all passed through the sea; And were all baptized unto Moses in the cloud and in the sea; And did all eat the same spiritual meat; And did all drink the same spiritual drink: for they drank of that spiritual Rock that followed them: and that Rock was Christ. But with many of them God was not well pleased: for they were overthrown in the wilderness. Now these things were our examples, to the intent we should not lust after evil things, as they also lusted. Neither be ye idolaters, as were some of them; as it is written, the people sat down to eat and drink, and rose up to play. Neither let us commit fornication, as some of them committed, and fell in one day three and twenty thousand. Neither let us tempt Christ, as some of them also tempted, and were destroyed of serpents. Neither murmur ye, as some of them also murmured, and were destroyed of the destroyer. Now all these things happened unto them for examples: and they are written for our admonition, upon whom the ends of the world are come. Wherefore let him that thinketh he standeth take heed lest he fall. There hath no temptation taken you but such as is common to man: but God is faithful, who will not suffer

"Hey, God"

you to be tempted above that ye are able; but will with the temptation also make a way to escape, that ye may be able to bear it. Wherefore, my dearly beloved, flee from idolatry. I speak as to wise men; judge ye what I say. The cup of blessing which we bless, is it not the communion of the blood of Christ? The bread which we break, is it not the communion of the body of Christ? For we being many are one bread, and one body: for we are all partakers of that one bread. (1 Corinthians 10:1-17, KJV)

No temptation has overtaken you that is not common to man. God is faithful, and he will not let you be tempted beyond your ability, but with the temptation he will also provide the way of escape, that you may be able to endure it. (1 Corinthians 4:11-13)

So Christ himself gave the apostles, the prophets, the evangelists, the pastors and teachers, to equip his people for works of service, so that the body of Christ may be built up until we all reach unity in the faith and in the knowledge of the Son of God and become mature, attaining to the whole measure of the fullness of Christ. (Ephesians 4:11-13)

Church

It's a word salad for the world. It's meat for Christians. I wanna drink the blood of Jesus.

> So from now on we regard no one from a worldly point of view. Though we once regarded Christ in this way, we do so no longer. 17 Therefore, if anyone is in Christ, the new creation has come: The old has gone, the new is here! (2 Corinthians 5:16)

> If any man think himself to be a prophet, or spiritual, let him acknowledge that the things that I write unto you are the commandments of the Lord. (1Corinthians 14:37)

> Let the peace of Christ rule in your hearts, to which indeed you were called in one body; and be thankful. (Colossians 3:15)

> Preach the word; be prepared in season and out of season; correct, rebuke and encourage—with great patience and careful instruction. (2 Timothy 4:2)

"Hey, God"

I didn't go to seminary, but if your pastor went for four or six years, his sermons are the result of his seminary education; therefore, you're getting a Bible college and seminary education for free. You should pay careful attention.

> Since we have gifts that differ according to the grace given to us, each of us is to exercise them accordingly: if prophecy, according to the proportion of his faith; if service, in his serving; or he who teaches, in his teaching; or he who exhorts, in his exhortation; he who gives, with liberality; he who leads, with diligence; he who shows mercy, with cheerfulness. (Romans 12:6-8)

> Do not merely listen to the word, and so deceive yourselves. Do what it says. (James 1:22)

> For where two or three gather in my name, there am I with them." (Matthew 18:20)

End Times

God loves the world for God did not send his Son into the world to condemn the world, but to save the world through him.

The Destruction of the Temple and Signs of the End Times

Jesus left the temple and was walking away when his disciples came up to him to call his attention to its buildings. "Do you see all these things?" he asked. "Truly I tell you, not one stone here will be left on another; everyone will be thrown down."

> "As Jesus was sitting on the Mount of Olives, the disciples came to him privately. 'Tell us,' they said, 'when will this happen, and what will be the sign of your coming and of the end of the age?' Jesus answered: 'Watch out that no one deceives you. For many will come in

my name, claiming, 'I am the Messiah,' and will deceive many. You will hear of wars and rumors of wars but see to it that you are not alarmed. Such things must happen, but the end is still to come. Nation will rise against nation, and kingdom against kingdom. There will be famines and earthquakes in various places. All these are the beginning of birth pains. Then you will be handed over to be persecuted and put to death, and you will be hated by all nations because of me. At that time many will turn away from the faith and will betray and hate each other, and many false prophets will appear and deceive many people. Because of the increase of wickedness, the love of most will grow cold, but the one who stands firm to the end will be saved. And this gospel of the kingdom will be preached in the whole world as a testimony to all nations, and then the end will come. So, when you see standing in the holy place 'the abomination that causes desolation,' spoken of through the prophet Daniel—let the reader understand— then let those who are in Judea flee to the mountains. Let no one on the housetop go down to take anything out of the house. Let no one in the field go back to get their cloak. How dreadful it will be in those days for pregnant women and nursing mothers! Pray that your flight will not take place in winter or on the Sabbath. For then there will be great distress, unequaled from the beginning of the world until now—and never to be equaled again. If those days had not been cut short, no one would survive, but for the sake of the elect those days will be shortened. At that time if anyone says to you, 'Look, here is the Messiah!' or, 'There he is!' do not believe it. For false messiahs and false prophets will appear and perform great signs and wonders to deceive, if possible, even the elect. See, I have told you ahead of time. So, if anyone tells you, 'There he is, out in the wilderness,' do not go out; or, 'Here he is, in the inner rooms,' do not believe it. For as lightning that comes from the east is visible even in the west, so will be the coming of the Son of Man. Wherever there is a carcass, there the vultures will gather. Immediately after the distress of those days the sun will be darkened, and the moon will not give its light; the stars will fall from the sky, and the heavenly bodies will be shaken.

"Then will appear the sign of the Son of Man in heaven. And then all the peoples of the earth will mourn when they see the Son of Man coming on the clouds of heaven, with power and great glory. And he will send his angels with a loud trumpet call, and they will gather his elect from the four winds, from one end of the heavens to the other. Now learn this lesson from the fig tree: As soon as its twigs get tender and its leaves come out, you know that summer is near. Even so, when you see all these things, you know that it is near, right at the door. Truly I tell you, this generation will certainly not pass away until all these things have happened. Heaven and earth will pass away, but my words will never pass away.'" (Matthew 3-35)

The Day and Hour Ywn

"But about that day or hour no one knows, not even the angels in heaven, nor the Son, but only the Father. As it was in the days of Noah, so it will be at the coming of the Son of Man. For in the days before the flood, people were eating and drinking, marrying and giving in marriage, up to the day Noah entered the ark; and they knew nothing about what would happen until the flood came and took them all away. That is how it will be at the coming of the Son of Man. Two men will be in the field; one will be taken and the other left. Two women will be grinding with a hand mill; one will be taken and the other left. Therefore, keep watch, because you do not know on what day your Lord will come. But understand this: If the owner of the house had known at what time of night the thief was coming, he would have kept watch and would not have let his house be broken into. So, you also must be ready, because the Son of Man will come at an hour when you do not expect him. "Who then is the faithful and wise servant, whom the master has put in charge of the servants in his household to give them their food at the proper time? It will be good for that servant whose master finds him doing so when he returns. Truly I tell you, he will put him in charge of all his possessions. But suppose that servant is wicked and says to himself, 'My master is staying away a long time,' and he then begins to beat his fellow servants and to eat and drink with drunkards. The master of that servant will come on a day when he does not expect him and at an hour, he is not aware of. He will cut him to pieces and assign him a place with the hypocrites, where there will be weeping and gnashing of teeth." (Matthew 3:36-51)

Acknowledgments

To my parents who parented me good and my lovely wife for making me a better man.

To Brandye Brixius a great author representative at Salem Media Group and the team.

And to love. Love bears all things, believes all things, hopes all things, endures all things. God is love.

We're christians, believers etc.

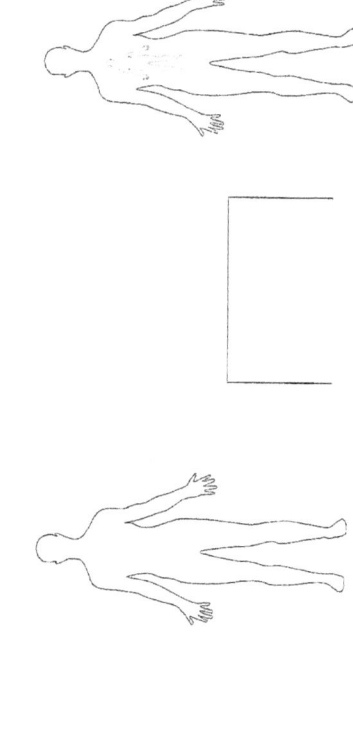

www.ingramcontent.com/pod-product-compliance
Lightning Source LLC
LaVergne TN
LVHW021743060526
838200LV00052B/3441